The Sand Dollar Cross

By

Lynda R. Burgman

To the best of my ability, I have tried to recreate events, locales
and conversations from my memories of them.
To maintain their anonymity, in some instances,
I have changed the names of individuals.
Copyright © 2014 Lynda R. Burgman

DEDICATION

This book is dedicated to my grandchildren and great-grandchildren and all who come after.

Our spiritual journey is revealed to us by "God Signs, God Moments" and sometimes by a "knock-up-side the head".
I hope your journey through life is filled with many signs and moments that you are blessed to receive.
May you find your purpose in life and live a life of purpose and may you have many great adventures in-between.

CONTENTS

AUTHOR'S NOTE

To all my priestly friends and spiritual advisors who have taken this journey with me, I express my deepest thanks. You have brought much comfort to this soul in time of questioning, angst, doubt and an overwhelming feeling of unworthiness. Through you and your guidance, the path has brightened and continues to shine brightly. God and "His Signs" show me the rest of the way.

PROLOGUE

On May 6, 2012 while on a flight from Cusco to Lima, Peru, a stranger, an Indian woman, leaned across the aisle and proceeded to tell me that she saw a brilliant, white light surrounding my body and that it was emitting love. "I see your spiritual aura," she said. That statement was the beginning of listening to her for two hours, as she told me why I had been in Peru, about my family, my children, my charitable work, my future, (which she said included the writing of this book) and about what she saw as my "spiritual journey".

I was confused, bewildered and stunned. I couldn't even begin to describe the feelings I had after listening to this woman named Manjeet. Any sane person would wonder: how could this be? How does a stranger come up to you on an airplane and begin telling you about your life because she saw a bright white light surrounding your body? How do you get on the radar of a spiritual woman who says she "channels?" Trying to find the answer to these questions sent me on a journey which began in my recent past and ended by helping me understand the future and my place in God's plan for me.

Like many children of my generation, I was raised "in the church". We lived in the country and the little rural Baptist Church my Mother and I attended encouraged you to attend Sunday morning service, Sunday night bible study and Wednesday evening choir practice. We were at the church three times a week and sometimes more depending on what activities were taking place. Plus, ten days each summer were spent at vacation bible school.

Most of what I have learned about Jesus, Mary, Abraham, Moses and the bible, I learned in that rural Baptist Church. In my twenties, I became a Catholic. I would not say I was devout but, I tried to attend Mass each Sunday and to follow the teachings of the church. The church was a place of great comfort and solace when I had to deal with my Mother's illness and death just two days before my wedding. Mass was and still is the place where I find incredible peace and joy. However, beginning in 2005, strange things started happening to me which I can only describe as God's "thump up-side the head" and my true spiritual awakening.

My husband and I had recently retired and moved to a rural area west of the city of St. Louis. In October of 2005, I read an article in the local newspaper stating volunteers were needed at a nearby food pantry. They needed people to help stock the shelves and hand out food to those in need. Little did I know that a simple phone call to that food pantry would be the beginning of a spiritual journey that would take me over 3,000 miles from my home to Peru, to an appearance on the Oprah Winfrey Show, to finding God's sand dollar cross, to receiving a Human Rights Award and ultimately to sit across the aisle from Manjeet.

Chapter One

Does God talk to us through "signs and moments?" Many people believe they come to us not when we want them but, when we are ready. St. Ignatius said, "Finding God in all things is possible." God *is* present in our daily lives. We just need to look for Him, to know He is there and to recognize what He has put in our path.

It has taken me many years but, I have finally realized that my life experience has been preparing me for my life's purpose and for what God has wanted me to do. For over thirty years, my career was spent in the non-profit world working for a large charitable organization. During the next ten post-retirement years, I was a consultant to a variety of non-profit organizations and charitable institutions throughout the St. Louis region. Throughout that time, I managed boards, fund-raising campaigns, international programs, leadership development and major construction projects. During those years, I also had occasion to travel to Europe and South America for my charitable work. In Bogota, Colombia, I spent time working with the "street children" and at youth camps, located high in the Colombian Andes. I worked to help impoverished children and their families. Through that experience, I became familiar with being in primitive conditions in the developing world.

In addition to being a wife, mother and grandmother, there is another aspect of my life that is a very important part of who I am, and it is key to this story. All my life, I have had this *need* to be in the woods and in the wilderness. It is a need to be close to nature and to experience outdoor adventures. This has been part of my being since childhood. For 13 years, I was an only child before my sisters were born. My parents could always find me hiking in the woods, exploring hidden caves or climbing trees. Over the years, I have canoed 700 miles through the Arctic Circle, summitted Mt. Whitney, hiked on many mountains around the world, camped in most US National Parks and experienced many great adventures in-between. It is in the wilderness that I find my greatest inner peace, joy and spiritual enlightenment. It is my sanctuary.

In 2005, my husband and I retired, built a home west of the burbs and settled into a life pursuing what we enjoy most. That included wilderness adventures for me and fishing for my husband. In October of that year, I came across an article in the community newspaper explaining the need for volunteers at the local food pantry. The Executive Director, featured in the article, indicated volunteers were needed to help stock and distribute food to the homeless and underprivileged. I called to say I would be happy to volunteer once-a-week. The phone rang and rang but, no one answered. I called again but, still no answer. I put the article aside and planned to call the next day.

However, the Christmas holidays soon came, and I forgot about the food pantry. One day a few months later, I happened upon the article and called. A woman answered, I told her I knew the article was old but, if they still needed volunteers, I would be happy to come to the food pantry to help. There was a long silence and then she asked if I could come to her office to discuss their needs.

Sitting in her office the next day she suddenly began crying as she began talking to me about my phone call. The first thing she said was, "The food pantry may have to close because we are almost out of funds". She continued to tell me their budget was depleted and that they didn't know how long they could keep the food pantry open. She said, "You are not going to believe what I am about to say but, the day you called, I was on my knees praying. I was asking God to send someone to help us raise enough money to keep the doors open. As I was praying the phone rang and it was you. The minute the phone rang I knew God had answered my prayers!" She then asked, "Do you know anything about raising money for a charitable organization?" Shocked, I nervously laughed and said I had spent the last 30 years helping non-profits. I told her I tried calling the food pantry months ago, but no one answered. "We didn't need your help then", she said. "God is sending you to help us now". It was a sobering moment for me. I asked, "Were you really on your knees praying when I called?" "I'm afraid so," she said. "You were sent here to help us!"

I began to cry as I realized God wanted me there, at that moment, in that place, to help those people. He wanted me to help the poor and homeless who came to the pantry each day seeking food. It was God's first "thump up-side my head".

I can only describe it as a true moment of spiritual awakening. I felt God was speaking to me through this woman. I was humbled and shaken by this encounter and it was something I will never forget. I spent the next few months raising enough money to help the food pantry stay open. I felt God's hand throughout the entire fund-raising effort and knew He had placed people in my path to help raise the funds. I was but a conduit for Him to help the pantry's poor and needy. I was humbled by the whole experience and felt this confluence of events was something more than a mere coincidence or pure chance, something categorically different was happening to me.

Later that same year, I turned my attention toward my next outdoor adventure, Peru. I have always had a list of places and outdoor adventures I wanted to take before I left Mother Earth. I guess it was my own "bucket list" before such a phrase existed. Over the years, I have had many adventures. I've hiked in many of the national parks, the Alps, Rockies, Sierras, Dolomites and summited Mt. Whitney, the highest mountain in the lower 48 states, canoed 700 miles through the Artic Circle and on the great Missouri and Green Rivers. I have hiked across England, Spain, parts of France and on glaciers in Patagonia and Iceland. Now, I was ready to go to Peru, I was going to hike the Inca Trail to Machu Picchu. I wanted to hike this trail for years. Who doesn't want to see the ancient ruins sitting high above the clouds in Peru?

Little did I know that the most amazing adventure of all was awaiting me there.

Chapter Two

The trip to hike to Machu Picchu included an experienced guide and several days of hiking Inca ruins around Cuzco to acclimate to the 10,000+ altitude prior to beginning the trek up the Inca Trail. On the fourth day in Peru, our group began the hike. I've hiked all over the world and I must say the Incas built one of the most difficult trails I've ever hiked. It was like climbing 3,000 steps non-stop on a workout machine. Saying it was tough, is an understatement. There were no switchbacks. There were irregular step heights, generally broken and steep rocks to climb over on most of the trail to the historic ruins. My eyes never left the trail for fear of falling. Plus, being 62 at the time, probably had a lot to do with the difficulty.

At one point into our journey, we passed ancient salt pools carved by the Incas into the mountainside to catch water flowing from the springs. The springs have a high content of salt and as the water flows down the mountain, the salt forms into a hard crust on top of each pool. Looking at the salt pools, it seemed as if snow had fallen, forming circles all the way down the mountainside. Spoiling this exquisite view were many women and small children standing knee deep in the pools. They were bent over, caked in salt, skimming the surface with their hands to catch the grains into a pouch in hope, I later learned, of selling the salt for mere pennies.

As I looked at these children, I saw their legs and arms were caked in salt. Their backs were bent over under the weight of the sacks containing the morning's work. Many of the women were pregnant or had babies strapped to their backs in the traditional Inca wrapping. The children, old enough to go to school, worked the salt pools early each day before walking two to three miles to their classrooms. Many worked in the pools all day and never went to school. They were the indigenous Quechua people who lived in the District of Maras, Peru. They were descendants of the Incas. These ancient salt pools were called: Salineras de Maras.....the salt pools of Maras. I felt overwhelmed at seeing these children. I felt guilty that I had so much and that they were working so hard for so little. I could see they were suffering as they slowly moved through the salt pools. It was in that moment, as I gazed at the pools, I felt God's presence, God's power, I felt God all around me.

I felt overcome with emotion and could not look away. God's love is a power that comes in and transforms a moment into something better. I knew God was telling me not to look away but, to help them. I knew God had placed me there to see the suffering of these indigenous children. He put them in my path as He wanted me to not just look at them, but to really see them. *To see!*

I had an epiphany in that moment and thought about St. Ignatius who knew that finding God in all things was possible. I wondered, how many times God had placed an opportunity before me to live my faith and to help others? How many times in my life had I looked but, did not really *see God?* How many times in my life did I keep walking on my way, unaware of the opportunity God put before me to live my faith? I knew I would never know the answer to these questions but, I also knew that my life would never be the same after seeing those indigenous children.

Our group eventually made it to Machu Picchu and viewed one of the most spectacular sights of the ancient world. Machu Picchu is truly one of the Seven Wonders of the World, an engineering masterpiece. I was awed by the beauty of the ruins and history of the Inca civilization that once occupied this mountaintop. But, seeing the children in those salt pools would not leave my mind, not that day, not that night....not ever.

The day after our summit, we gathered at the compound for a traditional Peruvian meal before leaving for home the next day. After dinner, a man named Mario brought alpaca goods to sell to the women in our group. A few days before, we met Mario at a small alpaca shop located near the salt pools. The shop was established by Mario and a group of impoverished Quechua women as a cooperative venture. Profits from the sale of the alpaca sweaters, scarfs and jackets went to the Quechua families working together in the shop. It was an opportunity for the women to earn a small income for their families.

While my friends poured through the sweaters, I pulled Mario aside and told him of my shock at seeing the terrible conditions at the salt pools. He told me many of the children get sick from constantly bending over the pools, of their salt-caked bodies, malnourishment, a prevalence of stunting and that many did not attend school.

I also spoke to him about my concern of the poverty I saw in the local villages, the lack of water, food, electricity, and conditions at the schools. Suddenly, I could hear myself saying, "I will help the children of the salt pools". I promised Mario that I would do something to help them. I felt overwhelmed at seeing the children and knew God was "calling" me to help. At the time I made that promise to him, I had no idea what I would do to help the Quechua children, nor what God had in store for me. I only knew I was being "called" to do something to help make their lives better.

Meeting Mario at the salt pools was a true gift from God. As a Quechua man raised as a child in the farmlands of Maras, he knew of the poverty and hunger these children experienced because at one time, he was one of them.

How do you know when you are being "called by God?" What does it mean to live with purpose and to live a life of deeper meaning? What is your purpose in life? People want to know what God wants them to do with their life. In the Bible, the word "call" is used most often to refer to God's initiative to bring people to Christ and to participate in his redemptive work in the world. This sense of calling is especially prominent in the letters of Paul.

Paul's "calling" happened while he was travelling on the road from Jerusalem to Damascus. He was dedicated to persecuting the early disciples of Jesus around the area of Jerusalem. In the biblical narrative of the Acts of the Apostles, Paul was on a mission to arrest the disciples and to bring them back to Jerusalem. It was while he was on that journey that the resurrected Jesus appeared to him in a great light. Paul was struck blind, but after three days his sight was restored. Paul then began to preach that Jesus of Nazareth was the Jewish Messiah and the Son of God. **Paul's influence on Christian thought and practice was profound. He led the way among many other apostles and missionaries who were involved in the spread of the Christian faith.**

Romans 8:28

"And we know that for those who love God, all things work together for good, for those who are called according to His purpose".

Your life's calling is what God wants *you* to give to the world. It may not be as dramatic as Paul's, but it is what you are called to do and to become. It is what God puts in your path. However, you must look and be open to seeing Him in all things. Purpose can guide your life decisions, influence your behavior, shape goals, offer a sense of direction and create meaning for your life. Every one of us has been sent here for a reason. No matter who you are, we all have significance in this world. No matter how rich, how poor, how young, how old, we are all significant in God's eyes and His love is unconditional. God loves you.

Often, we think that "finding our purpose" means discovering some great calling or, making a huge impact in the world like Mother Teresa. But, the very fact we exist means we have a purpose. Callings and living a life of purpose are about contribution and giving of yourself in service to others. When you are giving to others, when you are giving back to God, you are being purposeful. Whether you feel called to stop hunger and poverty, to shelter the homeless, to heal the sick and dying, or to help your home-bound friend or neighbor, all callings are about contributing to the world and serving others. Whatever it is that you decide to do, you will feel purposeful regardless of how much abundance flows back to you.

According to Oliver Wendall Holmes, "Every calling is great, when greatly pursued" and it is Robert Byrne who said, "The purpose of life, is a life of purpose".

Little did I know, that God was about to put something in my path that I had never experienced nor, would I ever forget.

Chapter Three

The next morning, as we left Peru, all I could think about were those children. After I returned home, the thought of helping them bothered me for days. In my mind, I went through the tried and true fund-raising events I had successfully coordinated in the past however, nothing seemed to be the right fit. Two weeks went by and still, I could think of nothing to do to help the children of the salt pools. I soon fell back into my normal outdoor routine, family activities and consulting work with local non-profits.

Then one day while hiking my regular trail in the woods, I began to pray. I prayed that God would give me the wisdom to find a way to help the Quechua children. I prayed that God would use me to make their lives better. Rain was predicted yet, I wanted to hike. As I made my way through the woods toward the final section of the trail, the skies looked threatening. I had been hiking and praying for over an hour. As I approached the last part of a heavily wooded area, I suddenly felt a calmness come over me and I felt at peace. Then it happened.

Suddenly, the woods began to brighten with light. The light got brighter and brighter until the woods glowed with an amazing brilliance, unlike anything I had ever seen in my life. At the same time, I felt a warmth and surge of heat come over my body. It felt as though I was hot all over. I don't know why but, suddenly I began crying and then started sobbing. At the same time, I heard and knew God was speaking to me. The words were not spoken out loud rather through my head. I had a sense of clarity and a "knowing" of what God wanted me to do. I felt showered with the knowing. *I knew.* I knew what I was supposed to do to help the Quechua children. I knew that I would help them for the rest of my life. It felt like I was being "bathed" in love. I felt that I was being washed in God's love and grace. It kept washing over me as I stood there and sobbed. I don't know how long it lasted but, it felt like a long time. When it ended, I was emotionally and physically drained. To this day, it is difficult for me to put into words what happened in the woods on that hike. All at once, I felt a peace, a calmness and tranquility as I have never felt before.

No matter how long that I live, I will never forget those moments. A decade later, I can still feel the same emotions I did when it happened, it was spiritual, humbling and awakening. Those feelings and that soul-stirring experience will be with me forever.

However, a few days later I began experiencing a tremendous feeling of guilt. Rather than celebrating this "gift of love" I felt despair and entered a great sense of unworthiness. I felt that God had touched my soul but, I just couldn't wrap my head around what had happened. Why me? I didn't understand. I felt so unworthy and so undeserving. I could not accept the fact that this experience came from God. I knew He was choosing me to do His work and help the Quechua children but, I also felt strongly that I was not worthy. I tried talking to my family but, no one understood the depth to which my life had been transformed, nor the depth of my emotions. My young granddaughter only knew that "Grandma talks to Jesus".

Throughout our lives, my husband and I have known many priests. For over 35 years, my husband worked for the Jesuits and during my years as a Catholic, I have had friendships with many of our Jesuit and parish priests. I scheduled an appointment with my parish priest, Father Matthew, seeking an explanation, spiritual guidance and help with the tremendous guilt I was feeling. I told him of my guilt and a deep feeling of unworthiness. I felt so humbled and unworthy to have received these signs from God. I felt a sense of angst that would not go away. His words were the first to soothe my soul.

"You're not worthy" he said, "None of us are. Not Peter, the Apostles, St. Francis, Mother Theresa, nor the Pope. No one is worthy. Yet, God loves us and chooses us anyway. God is choosing you to help those indigenous children. God doesn't always call the qualified, but he qualifies those called. Don't question this but, accept what you have been given. You are unworthy but, you have been called. God will give you the wisdom and understanding to follow His calling. He is using you to help those children but, it is God who will show you the way. He will lead you, follow Him. You have received a gift!"

When he spoke those words, I felt as if a huge weight had been lifted from my shoulders. I could rejoice in what had been given to me through God's grace.

Even today, I still feel a great sense of unworthiness and guilt but, I slowly began to realize that it was okay that God was choosing me, a humble, unworthy sinner, to help His children in Peru.

I was also encouraged by another discovery I made. A few months after my meeting with Father Matthew, I found there were other people who experienced a similar type of "spiritual event". During a PBS special hosted by the late Dr. Wayne Dyer, (an internationally known self-help author and motivational speaker), he mentioned a book entitled "Quantum Change" (When Epiphanies and Sudden Insights Transform Ordinary Lives), written by Dr. William R. Miller and Janet C'de Baca. I immediately purchased the book and found that the authors had chronicled a variety of people's "life changing events".

Through hundreds of personal interviews and by collecting stories of people who reported having what they called "quantum moments", they discovered there was an undeniable similarity among each person's experience. The common thread seemed to be a warmth or heat within the body, a "knowing" or hearing unspoken words and seeing a light or brilliance around them. In each instance, the "event" was life-changing.

The authors determined that the quantum moments were characterized by four qualities. They are vivid, surprising, benevolent and enduring. Some of the people immediately gave up drinking or other questionable behavior. Some left a bad marriage, gave up drugs or quit other negative activities in their life. The people in a quick period-of-time completely changed the entire direction of their life, they were transformed. In some instances, the "event" took place years earlier but, the person spoke of it with the intense emotion as if it happened yesterday. Like me, the details and events were never forgotten, the quantum moment never went away. I was elated to read Dr. Miller's book. I finally felt as if I wasn't "crazy". I contacted Dr. Miller to discuss my experience in the woods. After a long conversation, he confirmed my feelings, that in fact, I did have what he called a "quantum spiritual event" in the woods. The reading of "Quantum Change" helped me remember a story shared with me by a fellow adventurer, named Jerry. I met Jerry while participating with a group of other adventurous people in a 700-mile Arctic Circle canoe trip. We canoed many miles together in the Yukon Territories of Canada and north through the Arctic Circle.

Four weeks later we arrived at our destination in Whitehorse, Alaska. When you spend four weeks in a canoe with a fellow, you pretty much get to know each other's life story. After reading Quantum Change, I realized that Jerry had a "quantum change" happen in his own life. As we canoed through the Artic wilderness, Jerry told me he used to be an alcoholic. According to Jerry, he was literally a falling down, lay-in-the-gutter drunk. He tried for years to stop drinking but couldn't. Each time he thought he could get ahead of the drinking, he would go out for a night on the town with his buddies and the cycle would start all over again. He lost his wife to divorce and was resigned to the fact that he would die a drunk. One night, after a week of heavy drinking, Jerry was on his bathroom floor laying in bloody vomit. He told me he knew in that moment, this was the rock bottom of his personal hell. That night he thought he was going to die. In desperation, he called out to God to save him.

He asked God to help him and give him the strength he needed to quit drinking. Jerry told me then something happened. "Something came over me, I heard a voice. I knew no one was there but, I heard God speaking in my head". He said he heard God say, "I am with you, I will give you strength, have faith". Jerry said he *knew*. He knew at that moment, he would never touch another drop of alcohol ever again. Like Paul, he had been transformed. He knew God had spoken to him and that he had experienced a wake-up call from heaven.

The next Friday night, his friends came looking for him to go to their usual hangout. Jerry told them he had given up drinking and going out to bars was over for him. Of course, they laughed and tried to goad him into going but, Jerry held firm and stayed home. After that night he realized, he could no longer live in his hometown. The temptation to drink was too great. He was afraid he wasn't strong enough to remain sober and feared going back to drinking again would surely kill him. Not knowing what to do or where to go, Jerry placed his faith in the God he clearly heard say, "I will give you strength". As a carpenter, Jerry thought it wouldn't be too difficult to find work. He loaded his tools and few possessions in the back of his pick-up truck and headed north. Living in Minnesota, he hoped he would find work before he reached Canada. Many hours later and with an empty tank, Jerry pulled off the road to get gas.

While he was filling up his truck he heard someone ask, "Hey, I see a lot of tools in the back of your truck. You're not a carpenter, are you?" Jerry was surprised but answered, "As a matter of fact I am and I'm looking for work. Is there any carpentry work available in this town?" Unbelievably, the man told Jerry that he'd been looking for carpenters for months. He was supervising a big construction project in town and had been so desperate to find workers, he began spending time hanging out at the interstate gas station. He kept hoping that someone with carpentry experience would stop to fill up and amazingly, that is where he was when Jerry drove up.

How did it happen that Jerry ran out of gas at that moment, in that town, with a man waiting at the gas station to hire a carpenter? Jerry told the man his story, he had no home, no work and no place to stay. The man offered Jerry a room in his home and carpentry work until he could get on his feet. Many months later, with the good paying job under his belt, Jerry moved into his own apartment. He met a great woman, got married and became a loving step-father to her two boys. That was ten years ago.

As Jerry and I paddled down the Yukon River, he told me he has stayed sober ever since that night on his bathroom floor. He knew God had placed the man at the gas station to help him towards a new life. Ten years ago, his "epiphany" not only changed his life forever but, saved it. Having a spiritual epiphany opened my mind to those who have experienced the same "happening" as Jerry and I.

I heard the Reverend Ed Bacon, rector of the All Saints Episcopal Church in Pasadena, California, speak on the Oprah Winfrey Show. He spoke of an experience he had as a young child while in a grove of pine trees. He remembered, "When I was five years old, I was playing in a pine grove in South Georgia. Suddenly, I felt enveloped by warmth and a light. I heard or felt, in the deepest part of myself, someone saying, "You are the most beloved creature in all of creation".

Rev. Bacon continued, "At the same time, I heard that every person is beloved in all of creation. It changed my life forever and made me what I am today". He immediately knew this was all about love. He felt powerful love. Even today, he said, when he remembers this experience, it changes the present moment and he is once again filled with love. Rev. Bacon encourages us to be in the present, to be in nature, to listen to the God within ourselves.

According to Bill Wilson, the founder of Alcoholic Anonymous (AA), "During the early 1900's people who were severe alcoholics died". He had his own quantum moment while in the bottom of what he calls an "alcoholic pit". "I cried out to God and the room lit up with a great white light. I had a feeling of ecstasy and a new serenity. I knew at that moment I was free". Wilson went on to start AA in 1935, to save not only his own life, but many souls from alcoholism.

The stories of Jerry, Rev. Bacon and Bill Wilson show us their "quantum moment" led to a dramatic and enduringly beneficial impact, not only on their lives, but on the lives of many others.

Whether we find God in a quantum moment or in the face of a child working knee deep in a salt pool, He is there waiting for us to find Him. All we must do is look and see, as He is there in all things.

Little did I know another God moment was waiting for me in the form of an appearance on the wildly popular Oprah Winfrey Show.

Chapter Four

A few days after my epiphany in the woods, I began what I later called a "kindness box drive". Hundreds of boxes were donated from a friend who worked at a local box company and I mailed two boxes to every woman I knew. I asked them to fill one of the boxes with gently used or new clothing, toys and school supplies. The women were then asked to send the other box to a woman they knew asking them to do the same. My plan was to have all boxes sent back to me and I would then send one large shipment to Peru for the Quechua children.

A week into my box drive, my middle daughter, bored at work, decided to check out her favorite websites including the Oprah Winfrey website. As she was looking through the site, she found a request to the public for "people preforming acts of kindness". She quickly e-mailed them writing that her Mother was organizing a box drive to help indigenous children in Peru. Within a few hours, a producer from the show called to say they would like her Mother to participate in an upcoming show featuring people conducting acts of charity and kindness. My daughter excitedly called me screaming something about Oprah, a producer calling and saying I was going to be on the Oprah Winfrey Show.

What? Astonished and amazed, I wondered, who goes on a hike to the Andes Mountains of Peru and then ends up on the Oprah Winfrey Show? I couldn't wrap my head around this and once again needed priestly counseling to understand what was happening to me. I immediately realized this serendipitous event was another one of God's "thump upside my head". I became fully aware and finally understood that God was now in control of my life and leading the way for me to serve His Quechua children.

The Oprah Show, I attended with two of my daughters, was called "Oprah Winfrey's Pay It Forward Challenge" and included 300 audience members. Each person was given $1,000, a video camera and challenged to come up with an inspiring, creative way to use the money to help others, for charity, or a kind endeavor. We were told to video tape things related to our act of kindness and to come back to the show in three weeks to share our experience with Oprah and the audience.

Between the three of us, we had a total of $3,000 and three video cameras to use. During the three weeks between the two shows, I quickly realized I needed to make my kindness box drive official. I established an IRS 501(c) (3) non-profit organization I named "Kindness In A Box". The date was October 31, 2006. How was it possible that thirty days prior I was standing on the Inca Trail gazing at the ruins of Machu Picchu? Now, I was the founder of an official international non-profit organization. Not only did God want me to help the Quechua children but, He wanted it done now!

My daughters and I worked feverishly during those three weeks between shows. By the time we went back, we had collected over two tons of clothing, toys and school supplies. It was more than enough for over 500 Quechua children. The biggest problem our new little charity faced, was how to get everything up the Andes Mountains to Maras, Peru?

Throughout my non-profit career, people usually ran the other way when they saw me coming because they knew I would either be asking for money or something else to help a charity. However, being involved with the "Pay It Forward Show", I quickly learned the power of Oprah. Doors opened immediately just by mentioning her name. When I called Fed-Ex and explained I was involved with an Oprah Winfrey Show project, they immediately arranged to come to my home, load the boxes from my garage into a truck, and take them to the airport. All of this was done at no cost. They shipped everything to Miami where the boxes stayed in a warehouse until I could find a way to get them to Lima, Peru. Not knowing what else to do, I found the Miami Yellow Pages and started calling air cargo companies. Sure enough, God led me to Luis Valencia, the owner of a small air freight company named Arrow Cargo. I poured my heart out to Luis, telling him about the children of the salt pools and that I didn't know how to get the boxes to Lima. Without hesitation, he said he would fly the boxes at no cost to Lima but, he could take them no further. I would have to figure out a way to get them out of customs, through the mountains and to the villages.   Thanks to Luis, the boxes left Miami within the week but, once again ended up sitting in an airport warehouse. The boxes, weighing two tons, were now in Lima awaiting release from Peruvian customs.

After much research, a "corporate angel" paid the exorbitant customs fees and my friend Mario, from the alpaca cooperative store, found a trucking company to drive the boxes from Lima, to Cusco and then onto Maras. Amazingly, the Quechua children and their families received the two tons of clothes, school supplies and toys just in time for Christmas 2006.

My daughters and I went back to the Oprah Show within the original three weeks. It was wonderful to see the videos and the variety of ways each audience member decided how to use their $1,000 toward an act of kindness or charity. Our project was the only international endeavor and Kindness In A Box was born. It was amazing to me to think that in those few short weeks since I stood at the Inca ruins of Machu Picchu, an official international charity had been founded, tons of clothing, toys and school supplies had been collected, I had participated in the Oprah Winfrey Show and everything made its way to Peru, unbelievably at no cost.

Was this a coincidence? Happenstance? An accident? Synchronicity? People who have experienced quantum change or synchronicity know the powerful effect such an experience can have. Synchronicity is a concept which holds that certain events are "meaningful coincidences". They occur with no causal relationship, yet they seem meaningfully related.

Being asked to participate in the "Oprah Winfrey Pay It Forward Show" may seem to have been a stand-alone event that came out of nowhere or could have been referred to as a simple coincidence. However, linking it with the encounter at the food pantry, the spiritual awakening at the Peruvian salt pools and the epiphany in the woods made me realize that something beyond my control was happening in my life. Something greater than myself was touching me.

Chapter Five

When I established the charity, I wrote a simple mission statement: *"To provide humanitarian resources that support the education, health and well-being of the impoverished indigenous Quechua children and their families in the District of Maras, Peru"*.

There is a saying in the non-profit world: "no margin, no mission". No matter how wonderful your mission statement sounds, nor how worthy your endeavor, you need money to make it happen. The "Oprah Winfrey Pay It Forward Show" provided us with $3,000. With the generosity of my daughter's companies, many friends and family members, we began our new charity with donations in the amount of $7,000.

Even though the clothing, toys and school supplies were greatly needed, I quickly realized the children had a very basic need and it was for food. Many of the children I saw at the salt pools were malnourished and there is a prevalence of stunting. I found out that "stunting" is very common in Peru and Peruvian children are affected at a 16% higher rate than their South American cousins.

Throughout my many years of non-profit work, I knew one of the most important steps in achieving a charity's mission was to use the resources available within each community, no matter where the community was located. Also, it was just as important to develop trust between myself, the families and village leaders in each community Kindness In A Box served.

With Mario at my side as the Kindness In A Box Program Director, I brought together the leaders of the Urubamba Department of Education, the Mayor of the District of Maras, and the Principal and Teachers of the Kacllaraccay School. With their approval and help, the Kindness In A Box School Lunch Program began in early 2007.

Word quickly spread throughout Maras and within a couple of years, we were feeding over 300 students in four grade schools plus, many toddlers, mothers and grandmothers who "happened" to show up on lunch program days. Our staff rapidly expanded to include our cook Augustine, two young women and other volunteers who helped cook, set-up and serve the food. Miraculously, our cook Augustine, always made food available to all. No one was ever turned away.

Over the next ten years, Kindness In A Box programs and projects continued to expand to meet the needs of the Quechua children and families. We improved village schools by providing new windows, paint, bathrooms, school supplies and equipment.

Also, working with the Urubamba Department of Agriculture, a Kindness In A Box micro-loan program called the "Henny Penny Barnyard Project" was started for Quechua women to raise barnyard animals for food and profit for their families. Training was provided to each woman regarding how to raise and sell the animals at the local market. The women had to pay the loans back within 12 months and the money was then passed on as a micro loan to another woman. More than 100 women went through the program and amazingly all of them paid back their loans within the 12-month timeframe.

The best example of cooperation and use of community resources happened in 2012 with the construction of the Kindness In A Box "Kindness Center" in the village of Kacllaraccay. Maras Mayor, Miguel Morales and I developed a close friendship during his years in office and he gave his full support to the project. The Mayor provided the architect to supervise the construction, trucks to haul rocks for the foundation, construction materials, concrete and free labor. The villagers provided the land, free labor, dug up rocks for the foundation and made 5,000 adobe bricks for the walls of the building. A generous grant from the Dorothea Haus Ross Foundation to Kindness In A Box helped pay for the roofing tiles, windows, doors, paint, paid labor, and timbers for the entire structure.

The Kindness Center has been used for community meetings, Teen Nights, the school lunch program, adult trainings and as a gathering place for everyone in the village. A large greenhouse was soon built behind the Kindness Center to grow organic vegetables for the school lunch program and for use by the Kacllaraccay School. Also, greenhouses for 16 families in the village were built so that nutritious vegetables could be eaten each day in those homes. Other villages heard about the greenhouses and soon new greenhouses were built at three more village schools. Every year since 2006, I travel to Peru to see the children and make sure the programs are properly administered. Mario, our Kindness In A Box Program Director, is indispensable to the mission of the charity.

With each visit, it became more and more apparent that God was placing people in my path to help the Quechua children and their families.

Among the many Kindness In A Box projects that were achieved, a new "Kindness Medical Center" was built. Through a partnership with the doctor and staff at the Maras Hospital, medical care will be provided monthly for families in Kacllaraccay and surrounding villages. Also, a group of 25 medical professionals from the Goldfarb School of Nursing @ BJC in St. Louis will begin coming to the District of Maras to provide medical care in villages where services are not available.

However, in May 2012 amid this journey, one of the strangest, unexplained things in my life happened. I could only imagine it was synchronicity once again.

Chapter Six

I had been in Peru for my annual visit which included meetings with government officials, village leaders and many of the participants in the programs. Word was spreading throughout the District of Maras about "Mama Lynda's" charity, and many other villages wanted the school lunch program, school supplies, greenhouses, Teen Night and micro-loans for their women.

Meetings to expand our programs were very successful and I could feel God's hand leading me to people who could help the charity's mission. As I prepared to leave Peru that May, I was leaving with a feeling of God's love and a realization that He had opened all doors. I knew He would continue to lead the way. I was just His conduit. He was just using me to help those children and to expand the charity. I was reminded of what Rev. Ed Bacon, from the Oprah Winfrey Show told me, "Sister, sometimes all you need to do is to show up and God will do the rest". After everything that had happened to me, I believed he was right.

While sitting at the departure gate in the Cusco airport, I diligently began working on my "KIAB to do list". It helped to organize my thoughts as I waited for the flight to Lima. Even though many things were running through my mind, I was distracted as I could feel someone's eyes on me. I knew I was being watched, I looked up and caught an Indian woman staring at me. She did not look away but, kept staring and watching me. For the next hour, she would walk by and stare, sit and stare, stand and stare until finally, I felt the need to say something to her. I stood up and began walking toward her but, before I could say anything, the attendant at the gate announced the flight was ready to board.

I quickly gathered my things and walked toward the gate. I was anxious to get home and begin working on the needed projects for the Quechua children and their families.

Most international flights these days are full, and this flight was no exception. My seat was toward the back of the plane and in the middle of the row. As people boarded, I kept hoping no one would sit in the aisle seat so, I could move over and have more room.

Finally, as the last passenger boarded, the door closed, and I quickly moved. I was buckling the seat belt when I heard someone say, "Do you know why I was staring at you?" I looked across the aisle and there was the Indian woman. "Excuse me?" I said. "Do you believe in miracles?" she asked. "What are the odds of us sitting across from each other on this airplane? God has put us together for a reason. God put me in this seat to tell you what I have seen". Surprised I asked, "What are you talking about?" Incredibly, she responded by saying, "When we were in the airport, I saw a brilliant, white light surrounding your body. It was emitting love. I can see love surrounding you in this light, that is why I kept walking back and forth staring at you. I can see your light, I can see your aura".

As I sat speechless, she told me her name was Manjeet and that she "channels". She said she receives "guidance" and preforms "spiritual healings". She had been in Peru for five weeks preforming spiritual healings and "feels and hears things from God or a higher spirit". Manjeet told me, God was working through me to help the Quechua children and that my charity will continue to grow. "God is guiding you and you know all these things I am telling you. You have felt and have known His grace and love".

She suddenly stopped, looked me straight in the eye and said, "Your daughter is suffering in her life. She must turn to God as she will find strength and peace only in Him. All will be okay but, she will only find her way through prayer and by seeking God". I told her that one of my daughters *was* having difficulties in her life. Shocked, I thought how could she possibly know these things? What is happening?

"Have you ever written a book?" she asked. "I see that you will write a book about your spiritual journey and it will be read by many people seeking enlightenment. You will help people on their spiritual journey by sharing yours". "Actually", I said, "I have written two children's manuscripts but, they have yet to be published". Little did I know her words would ring true in just a few weeks when a children's book publisher called me. I had submitted my manuscript to them and they called to say they could not use it as they were no longer publishing children's books. They wanted to know if I had written anything of a spiritual nature as they were now publishing spiritual and religious books.

I was speechless as Manjeet continued to speak about my family, my work in Peru, my relationship with God, and that she could see I, too, have a strong spirit around me. I wondered, how could she tell me these things when I have never met this woman before in my life? What was channeling and spiritual healing? What exactly was an "aura?" Was I crazy? What did these things mean?

When we landed in Lima, we exchanged e-mails and she said she would keep in touch with me because she felt we had a strong "spiritual connection". "God put us together on that plane for a reason. Trust the spiritual guidance you are receiving from God as it is very strong and clear, I saw this in the light around your body, your charity will go from strength to strength and continue to grow. You are meant to help the indigenous children and your spiritual journey is only just beginning," Manjeet said.

As she walked to catch a plane to England, I stood dumbfounded thinking about everything she told me during the last two hours. As I flew onto St. Louis all I could think about was Manjeet and what had just happened. Questions kept swirling around in my head which increased my level of anxiety, confusion and disbelief.

Chapter Seven

Once again, I fell into a deep sense of unworthiness, and guilt. I did not understand what was continually happening to me. The food pantry, the event in the woods, the Oprah Winfrey Show and now a stranger on an airplane tells me details about my family, my charitable work in Peru and what's going to happen in my future?

I began researching "channeling" but, did not find answers and only became more confused. I once more sought spiritual guidance. I desperately wanted someone to explain to me what was happening, I needed to have answers.

Father Daniel, my parish priest at the church I attend near our vacation home, explained that there are people who have a heightened spiritual sensibility. While sitting in his office he explained, "It is especially true of people from India and the Far East". He told me there is "channeling" from dreams, imagination, intuition and that some individuals are perceived as having a "connection" to other spiritual entities. He suggested that I read the book "Interior Castle". It is a book about St. Teresa of Avila who thought of the soul as if it were a castle in which there are many rooms. This sixteenth-century work was inspired by a mystical vision that came upon the revered St. Teresa, one of the most gifted and beloved religious figures in history. St. Teresa's vision was of a luminous crystal castle composed of seven chambers, or "mansions," each representing a different stage in the development of the soul.

In her most important and widely read book, St. Teresa describes how, upon entering the castle through prayer and meditation, the human spirit experiences humility, detachment, suffering, and, ultimately, self-knowledge, as it roams from room to room. As the soul progresses further toward the center of the castle, it comes closer to achieving a higher spiritual level, a perfect peace, and, finally, a divine communion with God. This is all done in a mystical context and with the grace of God. Father Daniel felt the book would give me a better understanding of what was happening to me and to explain Manjeet's gift of channeling and spirituality.

My dear Jesuit friend of many years Father Walter, like others, told me to accept what was happening to me, to accept that God was working through me and through others. God was doing this to let me know that I am on the right path by helping His Quechua children.

Father Walter said, "There are no accidents when it comes to God and who He calls to do His work. A calling is God's personal, individual invitation to carry out the unique task He has for you. Throughout your life, God's calling for you will bring great challenges." He continued, "You will often have distress, frustration and confusion like you are experiencing now. But, remember, you can't succeed at this task on your own. Only through God's grace, love and guidance will you be able to carry out this God given mission. There is no denying that something spiritual is happening in your life. Have a willingness to see it, to listen to it and to accept it".

And then along came Father Luke.

Father Luke was my home parish priest and friend. We sat in the rectory as I began telling him my story. Once again, I began with the food pantry, the experience in the woods, the Oprah Winfrey Show and an hour later ended with my amazing encounter with Manjeet. He sat quietly, smiling and nodding his head in understanding. When I finally finished, he began telling me a story that he said he rarely shares with others. His story gave me chills. "Well, I am not surprised to hear of your experience with Manjeet on the plane", Father Luke said. "You see, I have had my own spiritual event happen and it was also on an airplane. A few years ago, one of my dearest friends from seminary died. We had been friends for many years and I was asked by the family to come to New York to conduct his Funeral Mass. I immediately flew there, spent time with the family and officiated at the Mass for my dear friend. It was one of the most difficult things I have ever done".

Father Luke continued, "It was a very moving and emotional experience for me. After the burial, I caught a flight home to St. Louis from New York. The first stop was St. Louis and Los Angeles was the final-destination. We boarded and while waiting for the plane to take off, a flight attendant came up to me and asked if I would be willing to change seats with a man who wanted to sit with his wife. Of course, I said I would". The flight attendant then said, "Come with me, you'll be moving to First Class". I immediately said, "Oh no, I can't. I'm a priest. I've taken a vow of poverty and can't be seen sitting in First Class. Are there any other seats? She told me there were no other available seats".

"So, to allow the man to sit with his wife, I changed seats and found myself, for the first time in my life sitting in First Class". Father Luke continued, "The seat next to me was empty and just as the door was about to close, a man came rushing into the cabin and sat in that seat. I leaned over, looked at the man and immediately recognized his face". Father excitedly said to the man, "Wow, you're the Angel of Death, aren't you?"

I soon learned that Father Luke was a huge fan of the hit TV show "Touched by an Angel". He was such a big fan of the show that he had every DVD since the show's premiere, all except one. He didn't see the episode on television, nor did he have a DVD of it. He tried to find it but, to no avail. He had no idea what the episode was about.

The man was surprised and responded to Father Luke by saying, "Yes, I'm the actor who has played the Angel of Death character since the beginning of the Touched by an Angel series. I have also been a writer for the show for many years and wrote most of the scripts". Father Luke proudly told him of his devotion to the show. "I love the show so much and have a DVD collection of every episode except one. I watch them frequently and sure do know you're the Angel of Death. I've seen your character on many of the shows". The actor asked, "You said you are missing an episode. Which one are you missing?" Father Luke told him the month and year of the missing episode.

The "Angel of Death" opened his briefcase, shuffled through some papers and handed the priest a script saying, "I think this is the episode you are looking for. I want you to have it and I'll even autograph it for you". Father Luke graciously accepted the script and for the next hour of the flight read the most incredible story ever.

As we sat in the stillness of the rectory, Father Luke said, "Unbelievably, the script described everything I had just been through. It was the story of two friends who went into the seminary together and became priests. It described my friend's death, many of the words I spoke at his funeral mass and at the gravesite. The show was a story describing my life! I was stunned, and couldn't believe this was happening to me", he exclaimed.

I found it incredible that we both had amazing spiritual events happen to us on an airplane. I asked him what he thought of that coincidence? He laughed and said, "I think God purposefully had this happen to both of us on an airplane because he knew we couldn't escape. Before this happened to me I questioned many things about God and my faith. After this event, I learned not to question anymore. I had a peace and a knowing just to accept what God was doing in my life". He looked at me and earnestly said, "You should do the same. Stop questioning, stop feeling unworthy and stop feeling guilty. Accept the grace that is being given to you, I have. Divine guidance is always there, these spiritual moments you have been having are there to teach you, if you pay attention, accept them".

I went home that day feeling much better. I felt more focused on the work I was doing with the Quechua children, on being a better Christian and on being a more kind and compassionate person. In Father Luke, I found someone who completely understood the "craziness" of the spiritual events that were happening to me. I had to laugh when I thought about God sending Manjeet to me and the "Angel of Death" to Father Luke, both on an airplane.

Father Luke helped me understand that God does indeed work through others, such as the Quechua children at the salt pools, Manjeet on the plane, my friend Jerry and Oprah, all to bring me closer to Him. I would soon find others who would cross my path in the most amazing ways and bring God undeniably into my life.

Chapter Eight

After hearing Father Luke's story, I felt a great comfort in knowing that others shared similar spiritual events and experiences. I was beginning to have a better understanding of what was happening, I began reading and researching more about these strange events.

I learned what one person calls a spiritual or religious experience, which could be an intense life-changing event, another might call it a simple prayer or moment with God. Some would call this phenomenon an "epiphany" or "spiritual happening". This event can be a moment of sudden or great revelation that dramatically changes you in some way. Many people who experience a quantum event or an epiphany feel as if they have had an encounter with the divine or feel touched by God's grace. Most people don't talk about their experience or boast about it. They instead are grateful, thankful and humbled. Like me, most have an intense feeling of humility and unworthiness, feeling no entitlement or deservedness. As in Jerry's situation, it seems that everything in a person's inner being changed for the better. Emotions, values, spirituality, sense of self, and relationships all change. Understanding of the past, present and future is different.

After my spiritual events, change in my life happened immediately but, with others change might take time. John Newton, the sea captain who wrote "Amazing Grace" was inspired by a transformational experience which happened while he was transporting a shipload of slaves. During a 1748 voyage Newton had a spiritual conversion when his ship encountered a severe storm off the coast of Ireland. Newton awoke in the middle of the night as the ship filled with water. Newton called out to God to save the ship, he was terrified that all onboard would be lost. But, the cargo suddenly shifted and stopped up the hole leaking water, the ship slowly drifted to safety. Newton marked "God's intervention" as the beginning of his conversion to evangelical Christianity. Yet, he continued to make several more slaving voyages before finally redirecting his life to become an ordained Anglican cleric. Even though he continued in the slave trade for a time after his conversion, he saw to it that the slaves under his care were treated humanely.

For the rest of his life, he observed the anniversary of the storm as the day of his conversion, a day of humiliation in which he subjected his own will to a higher power. "Amazing Grace, how sweet the sound" so, begins one of the most beloved hymns of all time. It is a staple that can be found in hymnals throughout the world.

While Newton's change took time, Anne Rice a famous author, wrote the best-selling series: "The Vampire Chronicles". She wrote the series until 2012 and then stopped. At that time, she acknowledged receiving an inner directive, or "calling" to "Write for God. Write for Him. Write only for Him".

Soon after this spiritual happening, she introduced the "Christ the Lord" book series. In her most recent work, a spiritual biography entitled "Called Out of Darkness: A Spiritual Confession", she writes about this intense spiritual conversion and re-embracing her faith. This was quite a quantum change from writing about the darkness of vampires to writing about Christ.

The late American psychologist, Abraham Maslow identified spiritual moments as having four characteristics:

1. Vivid - The experience can be intense, with extreme clarity and brilliance. Many describe it as a strong, rich, deep and distinct happening.
2. Surprise - Astonishment, amazement, wonderment, shocked, awed, stunned are the many words used to describe the experience.
3. Benevolent - People always feel good, left with a feeling of compassion, good will, unselfishness, generosity, being philanthropic, charitable and bighearted.
4. Enduring - It doesn't come and go but, lasts with you forever. You will remember the experience as if it happened yesterday.

Andrew Newberg, MD, director of research at the Myrna Brind Center for Integrative Medicine at Thomas Jefferson University Hospital in Philadelphia, is one of a new breed of "neurotheologians" studying the intersections among our brains, religion, philosophy, and spirituality. Newberg surveyed around 3,000 people who had spiritual experiences and identified a few common elements. In his book, "How God Changes Your Brain" with Mark Robert Waldman, he concludes that active and positive spiritual belief changes the human brain for the better. Also, many who have practiced yoga for thousands of years believe that it is not just a vehicle for physical exercise but, that spiritual growth can be achieved through meditation.

Just like Dr. William Miller in "Quantum Change" and Abraham Maslow, Newberg found there was a strong sense of what the person calls "realness". When you wake up from a dream, he explains, you know it wasn't real, no matter how vivid it felt, not so with transcendent experiences, which feel authentic not only at the time but years later.

My spiritual event in the woods feels as vivid today as it was when it happened years ago. My encounter with Manjeet was an awakening to a spiritual unknown. As crazy as it seemed, I felt I was awakened to the understanding that some individuals can "see" spiritual surroundings and feel what is happening to others.

Since our first meeting, Manjeet has continued to communicate "messages" she receives about me. These "messages or feelings" usually explain an event that is about to happen to me or events that have happened. She channels these messages while she is in India or England and I am across the world in the American Midwest. To me, this is an unbelievable occurrence and one that cannot be explained. I don't know or understand how this happens but, I accept what she is saying and trust her feelings.

Manjeet recently e-mailed I would meet someone with a deep interest in hiking and spirituality. She said, "You will cross spiritual paths. This person, a man, also finds spiritual enlightenment in the wilderness and specifically in the mountains". Unbelievably, the next day, while hiking on my regular trail in the woods, I ran into an older man who was bent over from the weight of a heavy backpack.

This trail is difficult and known as the place to train if you are planning a challenging hike. Over the years I've hiked this trail, I've met people who were training to hike to Everest Base Camp, the Appalachian Trail, the Alps, the Rockies and many other challenging endeavors. Not dreaming in a million years that this man was training for anything, due to his advanced age, I asked if he was. He said, "Yes, I'm training to summit Kilimanjaro". Astonished, all I could say was, "Wow"!

Soaring high above northeastern Tanzania, Mount Kilimanjaro at 19,340' is Africa's highest peak. It is one of the most popular mountains to summit with an estimated 35,000 hikers making the attempt each year. I could not believe he was training to summit this mountain which is one of the highest in the world. For the next hour, I hiked with him. He told me he was Dr. Robert Wheeler and that he was 85! Robert said he was the author of a book called "Mountains and Minds". The book blends history and psychology. He determined that combining history and psychology, indicates that people have a psychological need to have a sense of purpose and meaning in their lives.

He told me, "People want to know their calling, their purpose in life but, unfortunately very few find it". Robert uses his own personal mountain hiking experiences, from Mount Fuji 12,388' to Mount Whitney at 14,505' and others, to answer the question: "Why do people attempt and train to do these things?" He delves into spirituality as a personality trait and personality characteristics that contribute to health, well-being and performance, much like the body, mind and spirit connection.

As we hiked, he asked about my hiking activities and if I ever had a spiritual event happen while hiking. I laughed as I realized that this was the spiritual person Manjeet had spoken about just the day before. We hiked for another hour as I told him of my "spiritual adventures" beginning with the call to the food pantry. His insight and advice to me were very helpful. He said, "So few find their calling in life but, you are one of the lucky ones".

Through Robert and others, I have learned that calling and purpose are not static. Purpose is dynamic, alive and continues to be applied throughout your life. Everyone has a purpose, everyone has a calling however; the challenge is to find it.

A calling is unique for each person, yet every calling has different characteristics. It usually feels urgent and persistent, personal and tailored to fit a person's soul. It builds on one's spiritual gifts and is a kind of surrendering. It is both a challenge and a joy. Author C.S. Lewis wrote, "To follow the vocation does not mean happiness, but once it has been heard, there will be no happiness for those who do not follow". Eric Liddell, an Olympic racer portrayed in the movie Chariots of Fire, described his calling when he said, "When I run, I feel God's pleasure".

I continued to hike with Robert a few additional times during the weeks leading up to his Kilimanjaro attempt. Did Robert successfully summit Mount Kilimanjaro? Yes, at sunrise on October 2, 2014. On that day with his son by his side, Dr. Robert Wheeler age 85, established a new world record for being the oldest person to successfully climb Mt. Kilimanjaro, the tallest free-standing mountain in the world. The main reason for this effort, according to Robert, was to "Get another mountain climbing story for the second edition of my book". He continues to inspire all who know him with his vigor, positive attitude toward aging and spiritual wisdom. He recently told me he wants to go back and summit Mt. Kilimanjaro when he turns 90. Knowing Robert, I believe that he will.

Chapter Nine

In 2016, Kindness In A Box celebrated its tenth anniversary. While in Peru that spring, I planned a big celebration to honor ten years of Kindness In A Box programs and projects that had helped so many Quechua children and their families. The Mayor of Maras, Eriberto Quispe Tito, and all the children and families in the villages of Kacllaraccay, Mullacas, Misminey and Chequerec were invited to the Kindness Center in Kacllaraccay for a 10th Anniversary Celebration Lunch.

I wanted to begin the day, celebrating Kindness In A Box, by inviting everyone to attend Mass at the local Catholic Church in Kacllaraccay. Mario, our Kindness In A Box Program Director, contacted the priest on my behalf. We were told that, the priest did not come to Kacllaraccay anymore because the people there "do not love God". He told Mario that "they do not come to Mass to worship God" and most of time when he comes to the church, only a handful of people attend. He did not want to come to the village anymore. Encouraged by me, Mario persisted in asking the priest to say Mass. Finally, the priest relented and said he would say Mass the morning of our celebration.

Upon learning the news, we immediately invited all families from the surrounding villages to come to Mass and after have a small breakfast in front of the church. Early that morning, I walked from the nearby Kindness In A Box Kindness Center toward the church. Holding my hands were many of the small children of the Kacllaraccay School. As we got close, I stopped walking and stood in shock as I saw a huge crowd of people gathered in front of the church. There were too many to count. I was later told, there were close to two hundred people who had come to attend the Mass.

As I walked toward the doors of the church, I saw many of the Quechua families from villages that were located on the other side of the mountain. I knew that these families did not have a car and realized, the only way they could get to the church was to walk over the mountain. It was overwhelming to know that all of these people traveled to celebrate Kindness In A Box and more importantly, to attend the Mass.

The church quickly filled to capacity and many, who could not find a seat, stood outside the open doors. Before Mass began, Mario and other Kindness In A Box volunteers, gave all who attended a small wooden cross necklace I brought to celebrate the occasion. During the Mass and before receiving communion, the priest always says, "Let us give one another a sign of peace" and instructs all to shake the hand of those standing in close proximity. The spiritual symbolism of this simple act has been part of the Mass since the very beginning of the church and found in the Gospel of Matthew, where Jesus said, "If you are offering your gift at the altar and while there, remember if your brother has something against you, leave your gift before the altar and go, first be reconciled to your brother, and then come and offer your gift". (Matthew 5:23-24).

Immediately after all of us prayed the Lord's Prayer, the priest asked us to "Turn to those close and share with them your love and the sign of peace". As he spoke those words, as one body, everyone moved forward to embrace me. Within moments, I was surrounded by every person in the church, touching me, embracing me and showering me with their love. I began sobbing in reaction to this outpouring, I could feel their love pouring over me and continued crying. I heard others crying in the church as well. The priest stopped the Mass while this was happening, and it seemed as if it lasted a long time before he began again. It was one of the most emotional moments I have ever experienced during Mass and one that I will never forget.

The rest of the day was spent at the wonderful celebration in the Kindness Center with lunch, speeches, music, and dancing. Many months after I returned home, I could still feel the magic of those moments. One day while hiking in the woods, I had a revelation while thinking about that memorable day and those special moments during the 10th Anniversary Mass. I suddenly realized that, the outpouring of love and kindness I experienced was not for me. None of it was for me.......it was all for the priest! It was for the priest to see how many people came to Mass that day. It was for him to see how many people loved God, wanted to worship Him at that little church in the village, not just on that Sunday but, every Sunday thereafter. That day the priest was shown God's greatest commandment: Love. It was meant to open the priest's eyes and give him insight into the depth and breadth of the love the Quechua people had for God.

Months later, I was told, the Sunday after the Kindness In A Box Celebration Mass, the priest began coming to the church to say Mass. He has come almost every month since that day to say Mass for the Quechua families, to officiate at weddings, baptisms and funerals. I believe the priest had his own "God moment" and was showered with the love that filled the church on that celebration day. I also believe I was just a conduit for him to realize the people loved God and wanted to receive Him *every* Sunday.

Chapter Ten

Events continue to happen to me as God put people in my path to further confirm my spiritual journey. An unbelievable and humbling event happened in 2015 when I was presented with the "Church Women United, Inc. - United Nation Office Human Rights Award". Once again, I asked myself, "Who goes to Peru to hike the Inca Trail to Machu Picchu and ends up receiving a Human Rights Award?"

Prior to receiving the award, I had been giving speeches about my spiritual journey throughout the St. Louis Region, mainly to various church groups. I had been invited to give a speech at a local community auditorium to a large group of people interested in not only my charitable work but, in hearing about my hiking adventures. The speech was well received and as people exited the room, I handed everyone a Kindness In A Box Newsletter as a way to further explain my work in Peru.

A few weeks later, the President of Church Women United of St. Louis, attended an event in the same community auditorium. As she sat in her chair during the event, she noticed the Kindness In A Box Newsletter lying next to her on a table. She picked it up, read it and called me the next day to come speak to their organization.

Founded in 1941, Church Women United is a racially, culturally, theologically inclusive Christian women's movement, celebrating unity in diversity and working for a world of peace and justice.

I was honored to speak to the organization and spent several weeks speaking at various churches around the city the members attended. Later that year, I received a letter from the Church Women United stating I had been selected to receive their "2015 United Nations Office Human Rights Award" for supporting human rights and for my high regard for the dignity of others. I can't explain the feelings I had when I received that letter. It was so humbling. I was unbelievably honored to be considered as someone who served others and who held others in high regard no matter their circumstance. That fall I accepted the award, "For leadership service as a mentor and social activist in human rights and human development, an advocate for peace and justice with no boundaries of political system, country, cultural background or religion".

As I accepted the award, I thought of others throughout my life who could have just as easily been nominated to receive this honor. I thought of my Grandmother who took care of her mentally disabled granddaughter throughout her life. I thought of my Mother who often brought people home for dinner that she "found" on the side of the road or my father who brought home a young European man who was biking across America. He stayed with us for a few days to eat, rest and gain enough strength to continue his journey. My Aunt devoted her life to providing loving care to her Mother during her Mother's final years. There are many people throughout our lives who do simple acts of kindness, love and have compassion for others. I was fortunate to have had many role models while growing up who showed me, we are indeed our brother's keeper.

Once again, I thought, how does it happen that someone left the newsletter on a table right next to the chair the President of the Church Women United occupied? Just as the man was waiting at the station for Jerry when his truck needed gas, the newsletter was waiting on the table. Coincidence? An accident? Fate?

The word *coincidence* is used only once in the New Testament, and it was by Jesus Himself in the parable of the Good Samaritan. In Luke 10:31, Jesus said, "And by a coincidence a certain priest was going down in that way, and having seen him, he passed over on the opposite side." The word *coincidence* is translated from the Greek word *synkyrian*, which is a combination of two words: *sun* and *kurios*. *Sun* means "together with," and *kurious* means "supreme in authority." So, a biblical definition of *coincidence* would be "what occurs together by God's providential arrangement of circumstances."

Nothing happens by chance. All coincidences have meaning. This "coincidence" was so incredible that it left me stunned and humbled. I had stepped into the world of synchronicity. What happens in most people's lives is beyond their control. No matter how carefully you design your life, you cannot know how your life will be affected by a single random event such as a newsletter left on a table. One small detail can and will change everything. I call it "Divine Timing". It is the idea that everything happens at its exact right time.

I grew up in a small rural community during a time when life was simple. I never, in my wildest dreams, would have imagined receiving a Human Rights Award. It was one of my life's most humbling experiences.

Little did I know that God was about to give me the most amazing, spiritual and miraculous gift of my life.

Chapter Eleven

One of the most amazing spiritual occurrences of my life happened a few months after my meeting with Father Luke. Most winters my husband and I vacation with our youngest daughter and her family somewhere warm. This particular winter we went to Florida to spend a week in the sun. Each morning, after breakfast, it was our custom for the whole family to take a long walk on the beach. One morning we walked to the beach to find sea shells for the grandchildren to bring home.

In addition to the walk, regardless of where I am or what I am doing, I always make time for morning prayers. Each day the prayers are similar. They include a litany of traditional prayers and my own which focus on what is going on in my life or in the world. In addition, I always ask for blessings for the families in Maras, Peru and for the wisdom to help the Quechua children through my charity, Kindness In A Box. While in nature, I spend about thirty minutes in meditative prayer, and feel closest to God in these quiet prayerful moments. That morning, the beach was beautiful. The turquoise color of the ocean, the white sand and blue sky were all a blessing to see.

As we walked down the beach, the grandchildren ran in front of everyone anxiously looking in the sand for unusual shells. My husband, daughter and son-in-law were right behind them. I trailed far behind silently saying my morning prayers. As I slowly walked by the edge of the water, I asked God for the wisdom and guidance to help the Quechua children. As I said this prayer, my eyes slowly searched the edge of the water for shells. I was amazed at all of the beautiful shells but, sadly most were broken into a million pieces. Few were whole. I always look for sand dollars because they have a special meaning in my life.

My younger sister Nancy, died at age 33 of breast cancer. After a hard fight against the disease, she died leaving two small children behind. She loved sand dollars, loved their delicate beauty and fragility. She loved them so much she was buried with one by her side. Each time I see one, I think of my sister.

The sand dollar is also rich in Christian symbolism. It represents the birth, crucifixion and resurrection of Jesus Christ. It is a flat-looking burrowing sea urchin that lives on the floor of shallow sandy ocean waters along the coast of the Northern Hemisphere. After it is washed up on a beach, it gets bleached by the sun and looks like a large silver coin, such as the old Spanish or American dollar. This is the reason for its name. On the top part of a sand dollar you can clearly see a star in the center, which represents the Star of Bethlehem. Around this is the outline of the Easter lily, a sign of Christ's resurrection. At the edges of the star are four holes and in the center another hole. These holes represent the four wounds on Christ's feet and hands while nailed to the cross. The center hole, which is the fifth, represents the pierce wound made by the spear of the Roman Soldier. On the back-side of the sand dollar, is the outline of the Poinsettia, which is the Christmas flower. Finally, if you break open the sand dollar, five "doves" emerge. Unbelievably, there are always five and they are the doves of the Holy Spirit representing peace and joy. It is the most delicate shell and one of amazing beauty. I have always loved and collected them.

As I slowly walked down the beach, I watched the waves roll in and out on the sand leaving bits and pieces of shells. My eyes carefully searched for shells, hoping I might find a sand dollar, all the while praying for the Quechua children. Suddenly, I stopped and looked down at the sand. There were millions of small broken shells, pieces of seaweed and coral everywhere. But, there at my feet I saw it, lying gently in the sand was a cross.......a perfect cross.....a sand dollar formed into the shape of a cross! Small, brilliantly white, the sand dollar was perfectly formed into a cross!

There it was, appearing at the very moment I had asked God to give me the wisdom and grace to help Peru's indigenous Quechua children. In all of the oceans in all of the world, on all of the beaches and of the trillions and trillions of shells, the sand dollar cross lay at *my* feet. Humbled, I fell to my knees in the sand and sobbed.

Chapter Twelve

To me, finding the sand dollar cross at my feet at the exact moment I was praying for the Quechua children was miraculous. Washed upon the beach from the ocean amidst trillions of shells, whole and broken, was the sand dollar cross. This was incomprehensible to me. As I looked at a whole sand dollar and then looked at the sand dollar cross, I could think of no way that the cross could possibly be formed without shattering the whole sand dollar into a million pieces. To me, it was certainly made by the hand of God. It was a miracle. It was truly a "sign" from God, for only God could create such a thing of beauty, love and meaning. The moment I picked it up, I knew God was communicating with me. I knew God was saying, "I am here, keep helping my children".

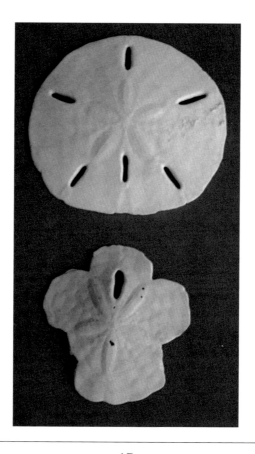

We all want "signs from God". Whether it's doubting Thomas, or Gideon's fleece, we want some measurable, physical arrow pointing us in the right direction in our lives. We want to know we are on the right path and making a difference. But, what is a miracle and how do we know it is God that is showing us the way through a "sign"? The dictionary defines a miracle, "as an event not explicable by natural or scientific laws. Such an event may be attributed to a supernatural being such as God, a miracle worker, a saint or a religious leader. Some theologians say that, with divine providence, God regularly works through nature yet is free to work without, above, or against it as well.

Many miracles are described in the bible such as the creation, Moses and the burning bush, the Ten Commandments and miracles surrounding the Exodus. Also, miracles surrounding Jesus include raising Lazarus from the dead, changing water into wine, Jesus walking on water, the resurrection and ascension to name a few. There are many miracles that are not in the bible, which include such happenings as in Lourdes, France and Fatima, Portugal. There are others that have been documented over the years including strange acts of physical strength, people recovering after being pronounced dead, hearing or seeing God and finding Christ's or Mary's image on various objects.

In a divine effort to wake up the soul, signs often appear exquisitely tailored to the attention of each unique person. The North Star spoke to the wise men but, the angels spoke to the shepherds and a dream spoke to Joseph. The most trustworthy signs come unexpectedly and without the asking and can strike a thousand different chords in our hearts from delight, amazement, knowing, to odd and even disturbing feelings. Can we ever understand how God's divine grace can touch one's life through a sign or miracle? The sand dollar cross was God's sign to me. Before finding the cross and during the months that followed, I received other physical and spiritual "God Signs" as well. However, no matter how long that I live, I will always think of the sand dollar cross as a miracle. I continued to be amazed and to have no real explanation for these occurrences other than God is somehow using me to bring others closer to Him and to serve the Quechua children in Peru. I stopped questioning and humbly accepted God's grace being showered upon me through these happenings.

Frequently, while hiking in the woods and during my prayer time, I continue to find "crosses" either left in the dirt on the trail or a "twig cross" lying on the floor of my garage to name a few. Recently, while hiking with friends in a California National Park, I saw a bright cross on the stump of a great redwood tree. All in the group walked by but, I was the only one to see the beautiful cross image upon the stump. I showed it to one of the women in the group, who knew of my spiritual journey, and she was as amazed as I was to see the cross.

I wondered, why was I the only one to see the cross on the redwood stump? Why was I the only one to see the suffering at the salt pools? I thought again of St. Ignatius and the core of Ignatian Spirituality. I realized that my growing awareness of God, learning to pay more attention to God, was opening my eyes to seeing and finding God in every place, in everyone and in all things. My eyes were opened to not only seeing God in the crosses put in my path but, to doing something about this spiritual gift. I realized that God is with us always and is a constant, active presence in our lives. We must simply open our eyes and look. He is there.

In addition to finding the sand dollar cross, one of the most meaningful crosses from God was placed brightly on the windowpane of my home. The afternoon sun was moving slowly across the sky, and at the exact moment I was in the room, the sunlight struck the corner window and formed into a perfect cross. Astonished and shaken, I quickly took a photo of the "God Cross". A couple of hours later, I went to church for evening mass. Unbelievably, the entire gospel reading and sermon that night was about "The Cross".

The priest spoke at length about Christ and the meaning of the cross in our lives. After mass, I showed the priest the photo of the cross on my window and told him that God had already showed me the message of the cross before I came to mass. Shocked at the sight of the photo, all he could do was shake his head, laugh and say, "Unbelievable, but yet, not surprising that He continues to show you these signs". I have not seen the cross since it appeared on the window the day of "The Cross Gospel".

The Christian cross is seen as a representation of the instrument of the crucifixion of Jesus. It is the best-known symbol of Christianity. Early Christians accepted that the cross was the "gallows" on which Jesus died and in the 2nd century, they began to use it as a Christian symbol. During the first three centuries of the Christian era, the cross was a "symbol of minor importance" when compared to the prominence given to it later, but by the 2nd century, it was so closely associated with Christians, that the body of Christian believers were known as "devotees of the Cross".

Paradoxically, the cross is a symbol of suffering and defeat but, also of triumph and salvation. The cross is the universal Christian symbol, acknowledged by all denominations as the single visual identifier of their belief. The cross of Jesus Christ is central to the Christian faith.

Another "God Moment" happened while I was on the same trail I hike to prepare for my more challenging adventures. For a few years, I've been drawing crosses, every so often, in the dirt as I hike. For some reason, I was compelled to do this. I felt that if I put that cross on the trail, it would remind others of God or might be helpful to someone along the way.

On that day while hiking, a trail friend Bob and I were talking about how beautiful the day was. A man came hiking up the trail and we talked to him for a few minutes before he continued on his way. Bob ended up going in the opposite direction while I followed the stranger up the hill. I caught up with him at the top and saw he was sitting on a big rock having a drink of water. I stopped at the rock and told him it was a good place to stop for a bit.

After a few moments, he looked at me and asked, "Have you seen those crosses on the trail? Do you know who is drawing those crosses?" Not knowing what the man's reaction might be, I simply said, "Why do you ask?" He then told me he had been having a tough time lately and on one day, he had been praying to God and felt that God had abandoned him. He said he has been in bad place and was depressed. He felt God no longer was listening, nor heard his prayers. He felt lost, alone and distant from God. He told me, he came to the trail to hike and to get away from his problems.

He said, while hiking, he looked down and saw the cross on the dirt trail. He explained, "It was in that moment that I knew God was there. I knew God had actually heard my prayers!" He told me he knew that God was telling him, through that cross, "I am here. I hear you. I will give you strength and I will walk beside you. I have always been with you". The man had tears in his eyes as he told me this. I began crying, reached out for him and said, "It was me. I am the one who drew the crosses". Then he said, "I asked you about the crosses on the trail because I saw the cross necklace you were wearing". He told me I was his angel. As I was crying I said to him, "No, I am not an angel. It was God who drew the cross and God used me to give it to you".

A few weeks later, while hiking on the same trail, I abruptly stopped, looked down and was amazed to see that someone had carved the sign of the ancient Christian fish in the dirt. I was stunned but, my immediate thought was, it *had* to be the stranger who told me that my cross in the dirt brought God back into his heart.

The fish's first known use as a Christian religious symbol was sometime within the first three centuries AD. The early Christians began using the Greek word for "fish" as an anagram/acronym for "Jesus Christ God's Son and Savior". The fish outline was a logical symbol for the early Christian Church to use as, not only was fish a common food of the day, but it was also used by Jesus during his ministry:

Mark 1:17 "Come after Me, and I will make you fishers of men".
Matthew 12:40 "Jonah was three days and three nights in the belly of the great fish, so will the Son of Man be three days and three nights in the heart of the earth."
Matthew 14:17 "And they said to Him, "We have only five loaves and two fish."
John 21:6 "And He said to them, "Cast your net on the right side of the boat and you will find some". So, they cast the net and then they were not able to draw it in because of the multitude of fish".

In the years following the ascension of the resurrected Jesus to heaven, the Christian Church grew rapidly. Christians soon found themselves victims of persecution by both Romans and Jews. It became dangerous to be known as a Christian. When two strangers met and thought the other might be a Christian, one would draw on the ground the upper half of the fish symbol. It was very simple to draw the two curved strokes and could be easily erased if danger appeared.

The following month while coming down the trail, I saw Bob, a fellow hiking buddy, and standing beside him was "the man of my cross". I quickly went over to them and asked the man if he was the person who had been drawing the sign of the ancient Christian fish on the trail. He told me he began drawing the fish sign right after finding my cross on the trail. He said, "You have no idea how much it meant to me seeing the cross you drew on the trail that day. I really needed to see it and to know God had not abandoned me but, that He was there for me". The man's name was Chris. Seeing his fish symbols on the trail bring me great joy in knowing that my simple act of drawing a cross in the dirt brought him closer to God. Now, his Christian fish symbol will be a reminder of Christ to all who hike that trail.

Chapter Thirteen

Carl Jung, the noted Swiss psychiatrist and analytical psychologist coined the term "synchronicity" for those haunting coincidences that we all experience....those moments when an event or happening is trying to tell us something. Others theorize that synchronicities can be people, places or events that your soul attracts into your life to help you evolve to a higher consciousness or to place emphasis on something significant going on in your life. The more "consciously aware" you become of how these meaningful coincidences appear, the more you evolve spiritually. Carl Jung also noted that the events we call synchronistic have a certain unmistakable emotional quality to them and are called: "numinous". Numinosity is that experience we have that feels undeniably and unforgettably in the presence of God. That is what I feel every time I see a "God Sign" or have a "God Moment".

Over the years, I have not only learned that synchronicity is real but, there is also something I call "God Moments, God Signs or Divine Timing". All of these God moments and God signs are also what St. Ignatius believed, that God could be found in all things. I believe that it is in those quiet moments that God puts a "sign" or someone in our path to help us live our faith, to help us serve others and to bring us closer to Him. I have been led to the realization that God continues to shower me with His grace and the more He does, the more I see Him in all things.

I know there are those, like me, who often need God's "thump up-side the head" to awaken our soul and to awaken us to begin our spiritual journey. We must begin, and we must continue, because at the heart of each spiritual journey is the understanding that *it is a journey*. Think about moments in your own life. Were there moments when God left a sign for you that you did not see or realize it was there at the time? Were you at a crossroad in your life and your life changed dramatically? Did someone or something completely change the direction of your life?

The day I stood on the Inca Trail and saw those children, caked in salt, working in the salt pools, I had an epiphany. That day, I stood there with several other people in our hiking group. How was it, that I was the only one who had an awakening? Why didn't the others see what I saw? I finally came to understand that, the moment was meant for me and for me alone.

Think of all the "coincidences" that have happened to you during your life. Were there answered prayers? God Signs? Unexplained moments? Divine timing? If you reflect back upon your life, you will realize there have been God Signs throughout. You did not see them in that moment but, they were there. They were just for you and no one else. As St. Ignatius taught us, "finding God in all things is possible".

After all these amazing spiritual "events" that have happened to me, I know that God is always with us and there are always signs around us to let us know that He is there. God did not pick only me to receive these blessings, they are there for all of us. They are there in each and every day and in each and every moment. We must be still to see and be quiet to hear what God has placed in our path. We must be open and willing to receiving what God puts in front of us. We must be willing to act upon God's signs. We must look around us and look for God in all things. He is there waiting for us to see. "For the gifts and the call of God are irrevocable"....Romans 11:29.

This is a natural progression of a person toward the understanding of God. None of us are perfect. I am a humble sinner but, I know that this is not the end of the story, nor of my spiritual journey. I know there will be more God signs and God moments. My deepest hope is that I will continue to see them, be blessed by them, be guided by their message and use them to bring others closer to God.

My spiritual journey continues…..

EPILOGUE

In late summer of 2017, Kindness In A Box completed renovation of an abandoned building located in front of the Kindness Center in the village of Kacllaraccay. The building was to be used as the "Kindness Medical Center". The medical staff at the nearby Maras Hospital had agreed to come to the new Kindness Medical Center once a month to provide medical care to the children and families in the village. It was easy to renovate the building but, the difficulty in starting this new medical clinic project, was to find enough medical professionals to come to the villages on a regular basis to provide medical care for the families. While the Maras Hospital staff would be a big help, we still needed more nurses and doctors.

One day in November of that year, a second cross appeared on the same window in my home but, this time, it appeared in a different spot. Nothing was said that evening at mass about "Christ's Cross" but, I realized the moment I saw the cross, that it was once again a sign from God validating my work with the Quechua children.

The morning the second cross appeared, I got an unexpected e-mail from a stranger. She was an assistant professor at one of the most prestigious nursing colleges in the country: Goldfarb College of Nursing @ BJC. Her name was Kathi Thimsen. In her e-mail, the professor explained that she was on the Board of Directors of a local non-profit charity, I had been helping. She happened to see my Bio regarding my non-profit career and my work in Peru. As soon as she read it, she contacted me to say the she would be interested in bringing a group of young nursing students, RN's and medical professionals to Peru to provide medical care to the indigenous population.

Kathi told me she had extensive experience working with the indigenous people in the Amazon of Peru. Through that experience, she was familiar with living and working in primitive third world conditions. Happenstance? Coincidence? Fate? Once again, it was the "Divine Timing" of her e-mail. It was the God Sign and God Moment of the cross upon the window.

Whatever you want to call it, whatever you want to believe, in April of 2018, a group of 25 young nursing students and medical professionals from "Nurses 2 Peru" spent several days in the District of Maras, Peru. During the Kindness In A Box and Nurses 2 Peru Medical Mission, 570 children, adults, students and teachers received medical care at five Quechua villages and at the Hospital of Maras. Everyone who participated in this partnership of Kindness In A Box and Nurses 2 Peru knew that this would be the first year of what would become an annual medical project to help the Quechua people.

Each day "God Signs" appeared from rainbows in the sky to the sign of the Christian Fish at one of the village schools. This was truly "God's Project".

One of the young nurses summed up the experience perfectly:

"This past week, I had the opportunity to go on a mission trip to Peru. To say this experience was life changing is an understatement. Going into it everyone had their own idea of what they thought it would be like. Let's just say, we quickly realized how fortunate we are. Even though we did not speak the same language, as our patients, their smiles, hugs, and tears told us everything we needed to know. "Love needs no translation".... 1 John 4:8

Shortly after the appearance of the second cross, another Christian fish appeared to me while I was hiking on a trail located across the road from my home. This trail is one that "Chris of the dirt cross" does not hike so, I knew he could not have drawn this ancient Christian symbol.

I had been hiking and saying my morning prayers, when for some unexplained reason an unkind act that I had committed years ago came to mind. I began praying for forgiveness for this lack of compassion and for offending God. I became emotional as I asked for His forgiveness. I looked down and there was God's Christian Fish lying in the dirt at my feet. I stopped and sobbed at the sight of it. I knew in that moment God had forgiven me.

How does it happen that the professor contacted me just as the renovation of the medical center was completed? Or that Jerry, my Artic Circle friend, ran out of gas and pulled into a station with a man waiting there to hire a carpenter? How does it happen that Chris hiked on the trail and saw my cross just when he needed it most?

Where did the second Christian fish come from that was lying at my feet the moment I was asking God for forgiveness or the Christian fish at the village school in Peru? How did a Kindness In A Box Newsletter, left on a table, lead to the Human Rights Award?

After all these years, thoughts, angst, and elation, my conclusion to all that has happened to me, is that our lives are full of meaningful events and signs which God places in our path. These signs, moments, and events are not accidental, nor coincidence. There is no area of our life that is not touched by God. There is no day that passes that God does not shower us with His love. There is no day nor moment that God does not show Himself to us. These signs and God moments can be dramatic, such as a cross shining on the window, a sand dollar on the beach in the shape of a cross, or simply the love that shines upon the face of a child working in the salt pools.

The question is: Do we look for God in all things and see Him in the things He has placed before us? Can we look back upon our life and see that there has been a clear path of events leading us toward our life's purpose, leading us toward God? Most importantly, what do we do with the signs and moments God gives us? Do we ignore them, deny them, or do we use them to serve others? As the late comedian, Danny Thomas once said, "Success in life has nothing to do with what you gain or accomplish for yourself. It is what you do for others." Martin Luther King Jr. asked this meaningful question, "Life's most persistent and urgent question is: What are you doing for others?"

An answer can be found in Matthew 25: 35-40: For I was hungry, and you gave me food, I was thirsty, and you gave me drink, I was a stranger and you welcomed me, I was naked, and you clothed me, I was sick, and you visited me, I was in prison and you came to me. Then the righteous answered him, saying, 'Lord, when did we see you hungry and feed you, or thirsty and give you drink? And when did we see you a stranger and welcome you, or naked and clothe you? And when did we see you sick or in prison and visit you?' And then Jesus answered them, 'Truly, I say to you, as you did it to one of the least of these my brothers, you did it to me'.

These moments are there and will be throughout our lives. My sincere hope is that this book and its many real-life stories will inspire you to awaken to those God Moments and God Signs in your own life. Look for them as they are always there.

Begin your own spiritual journey with the knowledge that God *will* be by your side every step of the way with His love and grace guiding you.

SECOND CROSS ON THE WINDOW

NOTES:

1. "Quantum Change", When Epiphanies and Sudden Insights Transform Ordinary Lives; Dr. William R. Miller and Janet C'Baca; pg. 14
2. Rev. Ed Bacon, All Saints Episcopal Church, Pasadena, CA. Oprah Winfrey Radio Show; pg. 16
3. Bill Wilson, Founder Alcoholic Anonymous (AA); pg. 17
4. "The Interior Castle", St. Theresa of Avila; pg. 27
5. "Christ the Lord Book Series", Anne Rice; pg. 32
6. Abraham Maslow; Britannica.com; pg. 33
7. "How God Changes Your Brain", Andrew Newberg and Mark Robert Waldman; pg. 33
8. Carl Jung; "There Are No Accidents", Robert H. Hopcke; pg.54
9. Robert Wheeler, "Mountains and Minds", pg. 34

ABOUT THE AUTHOR

Lynda Burgman, is a retired non-profit executive and non-profit consultant with 40+ year experience. She is an adventuress who believes in the peace of the wilderness. Recognized by the Oprah Winfrey "Pay It Forward Show" in 2006 for her humanitarian work. In 2015, she was awarded the United Nations Office Human Rights Award by the Christian Women United for her international work with the indigenous Quechua children of Peru.

Founder of Kindness In A Box in 2006, a non-profit charity that provides humanitarian aid for the education, health and well-being of the impoverished, indigenous Quechua children living in the District of Maras, Peru. Studied at the Art Institute of Chicago's Goodman Theatre and Southeast Missouri State University.

A FEW OF GOD'S SIGNS

Some of Lynda's Past Adventures

- Canoed 200 mile stretch on the Missouri River (Lewis and Clark Route)
- Kayaking 50 miles on the San Juan River
- Canoed 150 miles on the Green River through the canyons of Utah to Colorado River
- Four-week canoe trip 750 miles through the Arctic Circle on the Bell River in Canada's Yukon Territories, the Eagle River, Porcupine River and the Yukon River into Alaska
- Backpacked Grand Canyon (twice)
- Hiked in Glacier National Park (4 times); Canadian side hike; Waterton; Crypt Lake Trail
- 5-week journey on the ancient pilgrimage route: Camino de Santiago, hiking across Spain; crossing over French Pyrenees
- Tour de Mount Blanc loop hike through Switzerland, Italy, and France.
- Summitted Mt. Whitney (14,495 ft.) at age 62
- Hiked Italy's southern volcanoes – Mt. Vesuvius, Mt. Etna, Mt. Vulcano, Mt. Stromboli
- Hiked England coast to coast, from the Irish Sea to Robin Hood's Bay, 190 miles.
- Viedma Glacier hike; large ice field in Patagonia, hiking in Argentina around Mt. Fitz Roy.
- Hiked in Italy's Dolomites
- Alps hike through Italy, Switzerland, Lichtenstein and Austria
- Hiked Canadian Rockies, Banff and Lake Louise; in Iceland and throughout 21 of the USA's National Parks

27312176R00048

Made in the USA
Lexington, KY
30 December 2018